GASES
AND THEIR PROPERTIES

Tom Jackson

Crabtree Publishing Company

www.crabtreebooks.com

Crabtree Publishing Company

www.crabtreebooks.com

Author: Tom Jackson
Publishing plan research and development:
   Sean Charlebois, Reagan Miller
   Crabtree Publishing Company
Editor: Adrianna Morganelli
Proofreader: Wendy Scavuzzo
Project Coordinator: Kathy Middleton
Designer: Karen Perry
Cover Design: Samara Parent
Picture Researcher: Sophie Mortimer
Managing Editor: Tim Harris
Art Director: Jeni Child
Editorial Director: Lindsey Lowe
Children's Publisher: Anne O'Daly
Production Coordinator and
   Prepress Technician: Katherine Berti
Print Coordinator: Katherine Berti

Photographs:
Cover: Shutterstock: Carlos Caetano
Interior: Getty Images: Steven Puetzer 7b; **istockphoto:** 5b, 17; **Robert Hunt Library:** 7t; **Science Photo Library:** Library of Congress 14; **Shutterstock:** 15, 22, 26t, Nino Cavalier 6, Richard Semik 13t, Sergey Tarasenko 21; **Thinkstock:** Creatas 5t, Digital Vision 8, Dorling Kindersley 16, 26b, Hemera 27, 29b, istockphoto 4, 9b, 10, 13b, 18, 19, 20, 23, 25, 28, 29t, Photos.com 9t, 12, 24, Stockbyte 11.

All artwork and diagrams © Brown Bear Books Ltd.

Produced for Crabtree Publishing Company
by Brown Bear Books Ltd.

Library and Archives Canada Cataloguing in Publication

Jackson, Tom, 1972-
      Gases and their properties / Tom Jackson.

(Why chemistry matters)
Includes index.
Issued also in electronic format.
ISBN 978-0-7787-4229-6 (bound).--ISBN 978-0-7787-4233-3 (pbk.)

      1. Gases--Juvenile literature. 2. Gas laws (Physical chemistry)--
Juvenile literature. I. Title. II. Series: Why
chemistry matters

QC161.2.J33 2012   j530.4'3   C2012-906383-5

Library of Congress Cataloging-in-Publication Data

CIP available at Library of Congress

Crabtree Publishing Company

www.crabtreebooks.com 1-800-387-7650

Printed in the U.S.A./112012/FA20121012

**Published in
Canada
Crabtree Publishing**
616 Welland Ave.
St. Catharines, ON
L2M 5V6

**Published in the
United States
Crabtree Publishing**
PMB 59051
350 Fifth Avenue, 59th Floor
New York, New York 10118

**Published in the
United Kingdom
Crabtree Publishing**
Maritime House
Basin Road North, Hove
BN41 1WR

**Published in
Australia
Crabtree Publishing**
3 Charles Street
Coburg North
VIC, 3058

Contents

What Is a Gas?

Gases are all around us in the air. We breathe them in to stay alive. However, anything **solid** or **liquid** can also be turned into a gas if it is heated up enough.

Gas is one of the three states of matter. The other two are solid and liquid. Most substances are solid in everyday conditions. A very common liquid is water. Huge amounts of it cover almost three-quarters of our planet as oceans. Cooling water turns it into solid ice. Heating water turns it into the gas form, which is called water vapor, or steam (when it is very hot).

Ice, water, and steam are all made of the same ingredient. It is just arranged differently depending on the **temperature**. The temperature at which liquids become solids is called the freezing point, or melting point if going from solid to liquid. Water's freezing point is 32°F (0°C). The boiling point is the temperature when a liquid becomes a gas. Water's boiling point is 212°F (100°C). Every substance can freeze, melt, or boil. Even rocks melt into lava, although they would have to be dropped onto the Sun to get hot enough to boil!

This iceberg, ocean, and cloud are made of the same substance—water. The cloud (and air) contains the gas form, named water vapor, while the ocean is liquid, and the floating iceberg is the solid state.

4

So what is the difference between the states of matter? Solids have a fixed **volume** (the space they take up) and always keep one shape. When a solid melts, its liquid volume is more or less the same. However, the liquid can flow and change shape. It will take the shape of whatever container it is poured into. Gases are different. They have no fixed volume and will spread out to fill whatever container they are in. They can also be squeezed into a smaller and smaller space.

Ice cream is a mixture of solid ice and air bubbles—until it melts!

Dry ice (frozen carbon dioxide) does not melt. It turns straight into a gas, forming a white smoke effect. The process is called **sublimation**.

Investigating Gases

Some of the earliest clues about chemistry came from studying gases. One of the first things discovered was that even though they are often invisible, gases are very much real substances just like the solids and liquids we can see.

Until around 200 years ago, nobody knew what a gas was. The word *gas* was not really used like it is today. Instead, scientists described the gases they came across as "airs." Since ancient times, it had been thought that everything in the world was made up of four types of substances, called the **elements**. The four elements were earth, fire, water, and air.

Later, **chemists** found many other elements—and showed that none of the first four were actually elements at all. Instead they were made up of combinations of other, simpler substances. Nevertheless, when early investigators—wizard-like people known as alchemists—came across gases, they described them as different types of air. These airs were mostly invisible but they could be told apart by their odors, or smells, and whether they burned or put flames out.

One of the first people to notice that airs were given off by other substances was a 17th-century Belgian doctor named Jean Baptiste van Helmont.

Bubbles are gases rising up through liquids. They burst at the surface as the gas mixes into the air.

Alchemists were the first people to investigate substances. Many of them thought chemicals were controlled by magic.

He noticed that when charcoal was burned, the ash weighed less than the original fuel. He then burned the charcoal in an air-tight jar, and the weight after was the same as before. Burning had turned some of the charcoal into air. Van Helmont named this substance *spiritus sylvestre* ("wild spirit" in Latin). He also described it as a *gas*, a word he made up from *chaos*, which means "confusion" and "disorder."

Before Science

Alchemists used words differently than they are used today. Liquids that boiled easily were called spirits. Strong alcoholic drinks are called spirits to this day for the same reason. Earths were crumbly crystals, while harder solids were known as stones. Many alchemists spent their time looking for a magical philosopher's stone that could turn lead into precious gold.

These flames are super hot gases glowing as they are released from burning coals.

Discovering Gases

Early chemists did many experiments on gases, or "airs" as they called them. They found many types of air, which are now known to be some of the most important gases in the natural world.

By the 1750s, early chemists showed that invisible airs, or gases, could be released from solids and liquids. They all behaved in different ways and that meant the gases were entirely different substances, just as stone is different from metal and wood.

One of the first gases to be discovered was carbon dioxide. This was found by Joseph Black. He called it "fixed air" because it came out of magnesium carbonate crystals when he heated them. Nothing burned in fixed air—candles placed in it went out. Black also found the same gas was released as bubbles when the crystals were dropped in **acid**.

A few years later, English chemist Henry Cavendish found another gas. This one was produced when grains of **metal** were added to acid. Cavendish found that this air burned very easily. He named it "inflammable air," but we now know it as hydrogen.

Flames go out in carbon dioxide, so the gas is used in fire extinguishers.

Joseph Black discussed gases with James Watt—a Scottish inventor who designed powerful engines driven by steam. Steam is hot water vapor.

Multicolored Fizz

Sprinkle a teaspoon of baking soda into a tall glass. Follow this with a few drops of food coloring and a small squirt of liquid detergent. Repeat this process three times, using a different color each time. Using a long spoon, make a hollow in the middle of the mixture. Fill a similar glass one-third full of water and one-third full of vinegar. Pour this liquid slowly into the hollow. Soapy bubbles of different colors will erupt from the top. This is carbon dioxide being produced when the vinegar and baking soda react.

Vinegar and baking soda react to release bubbles of carbon dioxide gas.

The way gases seemed to be involved in fire got people thinking. Flames used something in the air—often described as "good air." When that was used up, only "bad air" was left. Many thought Black's fixed air was the same thing as bad air. For example, fixed air was found in the breath people blew out. However, in 1772, Daniel Rutherford removed all the good air in a large jar by burning a candle inside until it went out. Next he took out all the fixed air by bubbling it through lime water (the fixed air made this go cloudy). What was left behind Rutherford called "phlogisticated air"—but it is better known today as nitrogen.

Next, Englishman Joseph Priestley found that heating a mercury mineral gave off another gas. This was "good air" because it made flames burn more brightly. A few years later, Frenchman Antoine Lavoisier renamed this substance as oxygen, which is the term still used. He also showed that water was formed when oxygen and hydrogen (which he also renamed) were burned together. It was also Lavoisier who suggested that the word *gas* be used instead of *air*.

> Soda contains carbonic acid, which splits up into liquid water and carbon dioxide gas, creating a fizz of bubbles.

Fizzy Soda

Joseph Priestley invented soda water when he mixed fixed air into water. He found it produced a bubbly liquid that was very refreshing to drink. Priestley only gave his drink to friends for fun. However, a German named Johann Jacob Schweppe heard about it and set up the first soda factory in Geneva, Switzerland, in 1783. Today, North Americans drink about 180 trillion cans of soda every year!

Rocket Fuel

The most powerful space rockets are fueled by nothing more than hydrogen and oxygen. These gases are cooled into liquids so they take up less room in the storage tank. When the fuels are mixed, they explode, producing steam—and a lot of flames and heat. The super hot steam blasts out the bottom out of the rocket, pushing it up into the air.

Gas Laws

Scientists have discovered that all gases obey three laws that govern how their **pressure**, temperature, and volume are related. The three gas laws also help to reveal what gas is made of.

Chemistry investigates how simple substances, called elements, combine to form more complicated ones, such as wood, stones, and even living bodies. Chemists use science to uncover facts about substances by running experiments. Modern scientific chemistry started in the middle of the 17th century. One of the first chemists was Englishman Robert Boyle.

He did many experiments to show that the earlier alchemists were not using science to investigate substances. Instead they believed in magic and even used spells.

In the 1650s, Boyle used the latest air pumps to investigate the properties of air. One of his experiments was to suck all the air out of a jar to make a **vacuum**. He showed that a feather fell inside the vacuum just as quickly as a stone did.

This experiment 400 years ago sucked out the gas from between two half globes. The air outside pushed the globe together enough to hold heavy weights.

However, in air, the feather would float downward more slowly than the stone. Boyle's experiment showed that air is made of invisible material that pushes against the lightweight feather, slowing it down as it falls.

Three gas laws relate the characteristics of gases: pressure, temperature, and volume. Volume is the space the gas takes up. A gas does not have a fixed volume but always fills the capacity of its container. Temperature is a measure of how hot the gas is. Finally, pressure is a description of how hard the gas pushes against other objects, such as the inner walls of its container, or against a feather floating to the ground.

Steam locomotives are powered by hot steam pushing pistons up and down that then turn the wheels.

Balloon Jet

Blow up a balloon as much as you can— a long sausage-shaped balloon is best but any shape will do. Do not tie the end, but hold it tightly to stop the air from getting out. Hold it above your head—and let go. When you blow up the balloon, you are pushing gas in, and the pressure goes up. When you let go, the high-pressure gas inside rushes out in a jet that pushes the balloon all over the room. Works every time!

The first gas law is named Boyle's Law, after the great scientist. Boyle's Law states that the volume of a gas is inversely, or oppositely, proportional to its pressure. (We assume that the temperature of the gas always stays the same). Putting it more simply, if a gas in a large container is pushed into a smaller one, its pressure will increase. So, if the gas's volume is halved, the pressure will double.

Jacques Charles, who discovered one of the gas laws, also flew the first hydrogen balloon over Paris in 1783.

The second gas law is called Charles's Law, named for Frenchman Jacques Charles who discovered it in 1780. This laws states that a gas's volume is proportional to its temperature. Here, we must assume that the gas pressure always stays the same. So Charles's Law explains that heating a gas will make it expand to fill a larger volume.

The third gas law is the Gay-Lussac's Law. It is named for another Frenchman, Joseph Louis Gay-Lussac, who worked on the problem in 1802. The law states that gas temperature and pressure are proportional, as long as the volume stays the same. That means heating a gas inside a sealed container will also make its pressure rise.

The gas laws explain why a balloon shrinks when it is left in the refrigerator. Cooling air makes the air's pressure drop.

Warm balloon

Shrinking Balloon

A party balloon expands as you blow more air into it. The pressure inside is higher than outside, so the air pushes against the stretchy rubber to make the full balloon shape. Put one of these balloons—a small one would fit more easily—into your refrigerator and leave it for a couple of hours. After that time, the gas inside the balloon is colder and therefore has a lower pressure. That means it does not push as hard on the rubber walls, so the whole balloon shrinks.

Cold balloon

Gases as Particles

Scientists found that the best way to explain the behavior of gases was in terms of tiny moving particles. The smallest particles are called **atoms**, but mostly the atoms are connected into larger units called **molecules**.

The idea for atoms is very old. About 2,500 years ago, Greek philosophers named Leucippus and Democritus suggested that everything in nature was made up of tiny units. They thought that these units could not be divided into smaller sections, and they called them atoms, which means "uncuttable" in Greek. These ancient philosophers had no evidence that atoms existed. They just thought it was a good idea that made sense.

Few other people remembered atoms until 23 centuries later, when an English scientist called John Dalton found some evidence for them. In 1803, he showed that a gas always filled its container by gradually spreading out—only stopping when it hit the walls of the container. This process is called **diffusion**. Dalton found that when two gases were added to a container, they both diffused independently of each other. Imagine a yellow gas and a blue gas are added to a jar.

Gases are made up of particles that can move around in all directions.

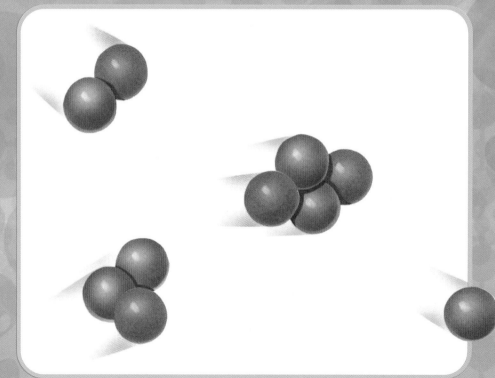

These smoke trails are spreading out into a cloud due to a process called diffusion.

They do not stay separate, with some parts being yellow and some blue. Instead, both gases spread out equally, eventually mixing together and forming a single green color.

The way gases diffused showed Dalton that each gas was made up of a particular type of unit, or atom. Our imaginary blue gas has different atoms than the yellow gas. Every atom is free to move on its own. They travel in straight lines until they hit another atom or the side of the container. Then they bounce off and travel in another direction. (The atoms in a solid cannot move and they make a fixed shape. In a liquid, the atoms can flow around but cannot spread out like a gas can.)

Our sense of smell relies on diffusion. The chemicals given off by objects spread out through the air before being picked up by our noses.

Dalton realized that not all gases were made up of just single atoms (in fact very few are). Instead the atoms are connected into groups called molecules. A water molecule has two hydrogen atoms (H) and one oxygen (O) making H_2O.

The way gas pressure, temperature, and volume are related by the gas laws can all be explained by treating gases as collections of molecules. Gas pressure is the push of the molecules against the walls of the container. Heating a gas (raising its temperature) will make the molecules move around faster. That means they hit the container walls harder and more often, so they produce a higher gas pressure. Squeezing a gas into a smaller volume has the same effect. The same number of molecules have less space to move in so they hit the walls more often, increasing the pressure.

Hot-Air Balloon

The first flying machine was a hot-air balloon, which took off from Paris in 1783. It contained a sheep, a rooster, and a duck, and it flew for eight minutes. All hot-air balloons fly because of the way the gas moves inside them. The heat makes the gas molecules move faster and take up more space than the cooler air around the balloon. Therefore the weight of the gas inside the balloon is lower than the same volume of cold air, so the warm balloon floats above the cold air.

The Air Around Us

We are surrounded by gases all the time. Our planet is covered by a thick layer of gases called the atmosphere. Without it, life on Earth would not be able to survive.

The air contains many gases but is mostly nitrogen and oxygen. There are also small amounts of other gases such as argon, water vapor, and carbon dioxide. These gases are held around Earth by gravity. All the gas molecules push against the ground, producing a force called atmospheric pressure. The air is thickest at the bottom of the atmosphere. As you move higher it becomes thinner, and the air pressure goes down. The temperature also drops, because thinner air holds less heat.

The atmosphere stretches up 400 miles (645 km). The bottom layer is called the troposphere, which is about 6 miles (10 km) thick. About 80 percent of all of the air is in the troposphere.

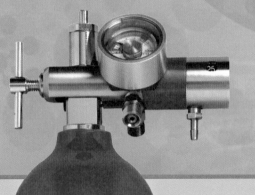

78% Nitrogen

20% Oxygen

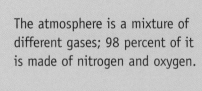

The atmosphere is a mixture of different gases; 98 percent of it is made of nitrogen and oxygen.

1% Argon

1% Others

The next layer is the stratosphere. Passenger jets fly along the bottom of this layer, which continues up to an **altitude** of 30 miles (50 km). Up there, the air pressure is 1,000 times lower than at Earth's surface. Next comes the mesosphere, which reaches to 50 miles (80 km). This is the coldest part of the air with temperatures dropping to –150°F (–100°C). Finally, the top 350 miles (563 km) forms the outer thermosphere. The gas is so thin here that most of the layer is in outer space. Satellites and space stations orbit through the middle of it.

Popping Ears

Ears pop when the air pressure outside the ear becomes different from the pressure in the middle ear behind the ear drum. It often happens when people travel on a plane. The pop occurs when air is forced into or out of the middle ear through a narrow tube that connects it to the back of the nose.

Wind is produced by differences in air pressure. The air rushes from an area with high pressure (a lot of gas packed together) to an area of low pressure.

Purifying Gases

Gases are found all over Earth. Not just in the air, but also bubbling out of the seabed or belching from volcanoes. However, they are always found mixed up and must be made pure before they can be put to use.

Liquid nitrogen is clear like water, but is much colder. Anything put in liquid nitrogen will instantly freeze solid.

Elements are the simplest substances. They cannot be divided into simpler ingredients. Most of the time in nature, elements exist combined together into a more complex substance known as a compound. For example, water is a compound of hydrogen and oxygen. However, a few elements are found uncombined with others. Most of these "native" elements are very rare, such as gold or diamonds (made of pure carbon).

The air is made almost entirely of native elements—the gases nitrogen, oxygen, and argon. These gases are all mixed together. The atoms are far too small to see, let alone filter out from one another. It is possible to remove oxygen or nitrogen from the air by reacting them with other elements. However, that process would have to be reversed somehow to produce pure samples of those gases in a complicated procedure.

The simplest way of purifying the gases in the air is to liquify them. Cooling a gas makes it condense into a liquid—the opposite of boiling. The gases in the air have very low boiling points, so the air must be made very cold for the process to work. At −297°F (−183°C), oxygen becomes a liquid. Only this gas **condenses** at this temperature so scientists can be certain whether a liquid is pure oxygen. Next is nitrogen, and only when it is much much colder does the argon liquify.

Helium, neon, and other rare but useful gases are purified using this system, too. Other gases are purified in factories, where chemical **reactions** are used to release them from **compounds**. Carbon dioxide is collected by heating limestone—similar to the method used by Joseph Black in the 1750s.

A gasworks, or factory where gas is made, is filled with super-strong pipes used for carrying gases at very high pressures and temperatures.

Using Gases

Gases have many applications. They can be used as useful chemicals, such as the gases that add the fizz to drinks, or they can be used for their physical properties, such as for powering engines or cooling refrigerators.

The chemical uses of gases are very varied. Carbon dioxide provides the bubbles in sparkling sodas. This involves a simple reversible reaction—one that can run in both directions. First, the carbon dioxide is mixed with water. The two compounds react to produce small amounts of a weak acid called carbonic acid. This is a safe, colorless, and tasteless substance that stays mixed with the water when the lid of the soda bottle is on tight. When the lid is removed, the reaction begins to run in the other direction. The carbonic acid breaks apart into water and carbon dioxide, which then bubbles out of the drink, giving it a refreshing fizz.

Heated oxygen is blasted through molten iron to burn away any impurities and make very pure metal.

> Aerosol cans work by spraying tiny droplets of liquid or a fine powder mixed into a jet of gas.

A similar gas called carbon monoxide is also an essential ingredient in extracting iron from its ore, or rocks that contain compounds of iron and oxygen. During the process, which is called smelting, the ore is heated with burning coal. Coal is mainly carbon and produces carbon monoxide when heated in a special furnace. The carbon monoxide needs oxygen to form carbon dioxide. So the gas takes it from the oxygen in the ore compound, and leaves behind pure iron.

Gases such as **methane** and hydrogen can be burned as fuels. A fuel is a substance that releases a lot of heat when it burns, and fuels also produce waste gases, such as carbon dioxide and water vapor. Internal-combustion engines, like those used in cars and aircraft, use these hot, fast-moving gases to create motion.

Ozone Hole

For many years, the gas used in aerosol cans was called CFC, short for chlorofluorocarbon. This complex gas was thought to be a very safe substance, safe enough to spray into the air without causing problems. However, in the 1970s, it was found that CFCs damaged the ozone layer. This is a thin layer of special oxygen in the atmosphere that shields us from harmful rays coming from the Sun. CFCs made a dangerous hole in the ozone layer. CFCs are now banned and the ozone hole is getting smaller.

The gas laws tell us that a hot gas has a high pressure, so the fuel in an engine is burned inside small chambers. As it burns, the fuel releases hot exhaust gases, which push against the engine's moving parts. In the case of a car engine, the chambers contain a moveable piston that is pumped up and down by the pressure of the gases. This motion is transferred by gears and driveshafts to the wheels, rolling the car forward.

In a jet engine, the exhaust gas spins a fan-like turbine, which creates a blast of exhaust that thrusts the aircraft forward. A similar gas turbine system is used in power plants to turn electricity generators.

Air is pumped at very high pressures into car tires to make them firm.

Refrigerator

Gases are used to make a refrigerator cold. The gas runs through a loop of pipes on the back. Inside the pipes, the gas is squeezed so much that it turns into a liquid. This liquid is warm and gives off heat, making the back of the refrigerator hot. The liquid is then squirted through a tiny hole, which makes it expand back into a gas. That makes the gas cold and chills the food inside the refrigerator. This process is repeated to keep food fresh.

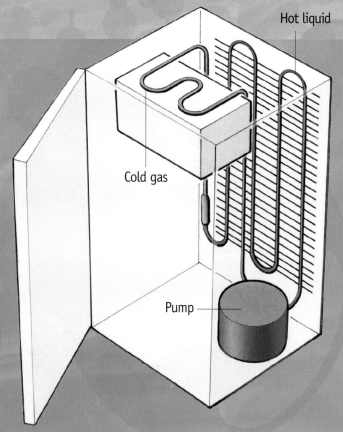

Hot liquid

Cold gas

Pump

A scuba diver carries a tank of liquified air on his back. Valves turn it back into gas before he breathes it in.

Greenhouse Gases

Many of the things that humans do release gases into the air, changing the makeup of the atmosphere. For more than a century, experts have warned these extra gases would make the atmosphere warmer and change the climate.

Without its layer of gas, or atmosphere, conditions on Earth would be much more extreme. During the day, strong sunlight would bake the surface. At night, the temperature would plunge to well below freezing. Thanks to the atmosphere, Earth's temperature does not vary that much. Light from the Sun shines through the air, warming the sea and land. The surface of Earth gives off heat, which travels back up into the sky. Some of it escapes into space, but the rest is trapped by the gases in the air. This trapped heat keeps Earth warm, stopping the oceans from freezing over and making it possible for life to survive here. This warming is called the greenhouse effect, because the gases are working like the glass in a greenhouse.

Greenhouse gases released by human activities will warm the whole planet. That will produce more extreme weather of all kinds. The extreme weather could be long dry periods, or droughts, stronger storm winds, and record-breaking floods.

The main greenhouse gas that traps the heat is carbon dioxide. Water vapor and methane also play a part. (Oxygen and nitrogen are not involved.) Over the last 250 years, the amount of carbon dioxide in the atmosphere has gone up by one-quarter. This is because we have been burning huge amounts of fossil fuels, such as gasoline and natural gas, to power our engines or make electricity. These fuels are the remains of ancient trees and other life forms that have been buried underground for millions of years.

Coal is a carbon-rich rock. When it burns, it releases heat and carbon dioxide.

Burning these fuels releases ever more carbon dioxide gas and boosts the greenhouse effect. Although the whole planet is warming only very slightly, that is enough to change the climate. Scientists say we need new sources of energy, such as solar or tidal power, to keep the climate from changing even more.

Power plants produce a large amount of greenhouse gases. Cleaner ways of making electricity are needed.

Glossary

acid A reactive substance that contains hydrogen. Acids often give off gases during reactions. For example, hydrogen is released when acids react with metals.

altitude The height of an object above the surface of Earth

atom The smallest unit of an element

chemist A scientist who studies the elements and figures out how substances are formed from combinations of atoms

compound A substance made up of two or more elements that have combined during a chemical reaction

condense The process in which a gas turns into a liquid

diffusion The process that makes gases (and liquids) gradually spread out as their atoms and molecules move around in all directions

element A simple natural substance that cannot be broken down into any other substances

gas The state of matter where a substance is made up of small units that move independently of each other in all directions; steam is the gas form of water

lead A very heavy but common and inexpensive metal

liquid The state of matter in which a substance is made up of small units that are connected together but can flow around each other. Liquids have a fixed volume but no fixed shape

metal An element that is a hard and shiny solid; metal elements have atoms with only a few outer electrons

methane Also known as natural gas, this is a compound of carbon and hydrogen that burns easily and is used as a fuel

molecule A combination of atoms that are arranged in a certain way

pressure A measure that compares the strength of a force to the area that it is pushing against

react To undergo a chemical process in which the atoms in substances are rearranged, creating new compounds or splitting them into pure elements

solid The state of matter in which a substance is made up of small units that are all locked together. A solid has a fixed volume and fixed shape

sublimation When a solid turns into a gas without melting into a liquid first

temperature A measure of how much energy is contained in a substance. At higher temperatures, the molecules in gases move faster.

vacuum When all the gas has been sucked out from a space

volume The space a substance takes up

Index

Web Finder

http://www.mhhe.com/physsci/chemistry/
  essentialchemistry/flash/gasesv6.swf

http://climate.nasa.gov/kids/bigQuestions/
  greenhouseEffect/

32